Frank the Farmer

Felicity Brooks

Illustrated by Jo Litchfield

Designed by Nickey Butler

Agricultural consultant: Liza Dibble

It's a sunny morning on
Hillfield Farm. Frank the Farmer
has already been busy for hours
milking all his cows.

"Off you go, Bluebell," he says,
sending the last cow back to the field.
"It's time for my breakfast."

Dairy

"Moooo!"
says Bluebell.

2

Frank's job is to keep animals for milk, meat, eggs and wool. He likes being a farmer but often wishes he didn't have to get up so early – or milk the cows twice a day.

Cowshed

Milking shed

Silo

Calf house

The milk is stored in the dairy until a milk tanker collects it.

Frank has some helpers on the farm.

This is Joe the shepherd. He looks after the sheep and lambs. Megan the sheepdog helps him.

This is Becky. She's staying on the farm to help with the new lambs. She's learning to be a farmer at college.

Frank lives in a big farmhouse with his family. Everyone's at home today as it's the weekend.

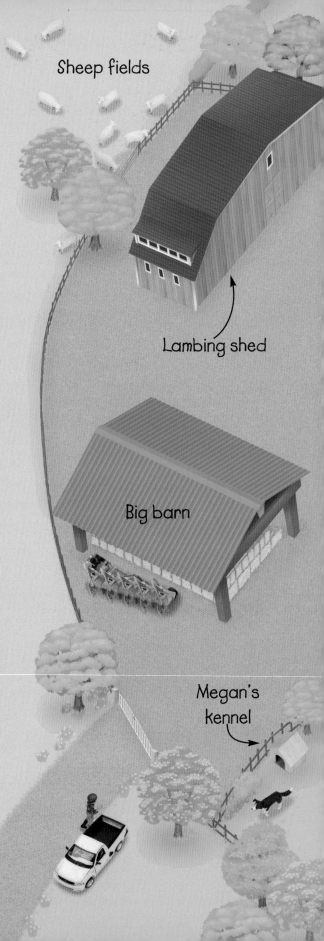

Sheep fields

Lambing shed

Big barn

Megan's kennel

Here's Rosie, Frank's wife. She runs a Bed and Breakfast in the farmhouse.

This is Olly chasing ducks. Olly is just 2. He likes making animal noises.

This is Emily riding her pony Misty. Emily is 10. She likes taking care of the hens.

Here's Lewis helping to feed one of the new lambs. Lewis is nearly 8.

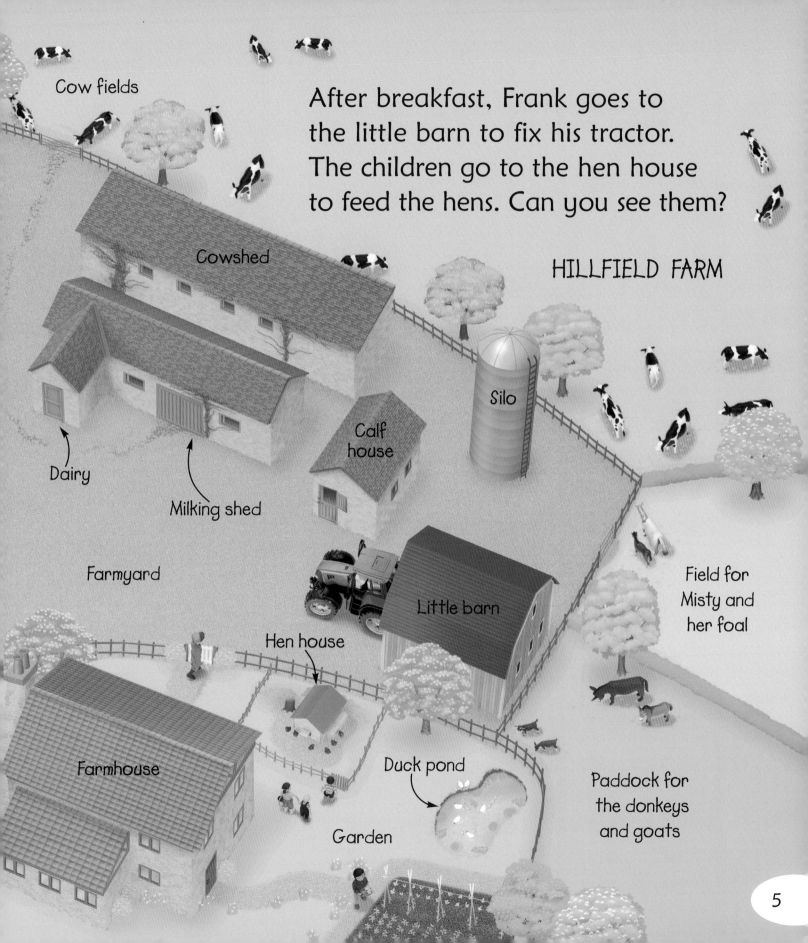

Cow fields

After breakfast, Frank goes to the little barn to fix his tractor. The children go to the hen house to feed the hens. Can you see them?

HILLFIELD FARM

Cowshed

Silo

Calf house

Dairy

Milking shed

Farmyard

Field for Misty and her foal

Little barn

Hen house

Farmhouse

Duck pond

Paddock for the donkeys and goats

Garden

5

Emily is worried.
"I wonder where Clarice is," she says. "I haven't seen her for ages." Clarice is Emily's special hen.
"Maybe a fox got her," says Lewis.
Emily looks sad.

"Brrrm, brrrm truck!"
shouts Olly.

A big milk tanker rumbles into the farmyard.

This tank keeps all the milk cool and fresh.

The milk from the dairy is sucked into the tank through this hose.

The tanker comes to the farm every day to collect the milk.

After a few more jobs, it's time for lunch.

"The Owens are coming to stay at the B&B this afternoon," says Rosie. "They have six-year-old twins named Rachel and Robert. Their dad says they're a bit of a handful."

"What does 'handful' mean?" asks Lewis.
"A little naughty," whispers Emily.

After lunch, Frank starts a messy job with the tractor, cleaning up the muck from the cowshed.

Squelch

The children go to help feed the new lambs.

"Baaaa!" shouts Olly to the lambs.

"Wash your hands when you've finished," Becky tells them.

Just then a car pulls into the farmyard. Two small children scramble out and start running around.

"Hello," says Frank. "You must be the Owens. If you go to the house, my wife Rosie will take care of you."

"Please don't run in the farmyard," calls Becky. "We don't want any accidents!"

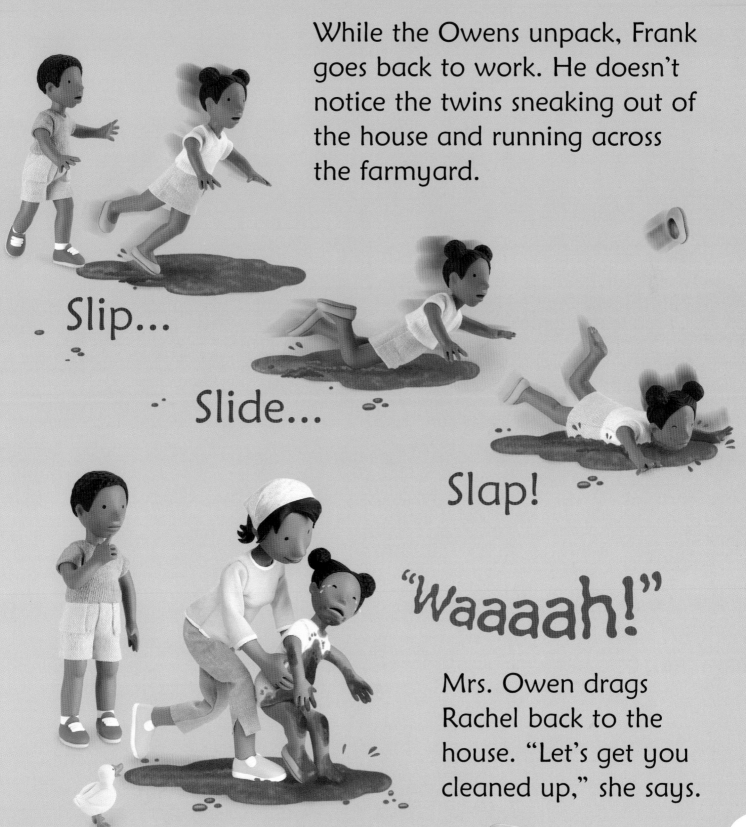

While the Owens unpack, Frank goes back to work. He doesn't notice the twins sneaking out of the house and running across the farmyard.

Slip...

Slide...

Slap!

"Waaaah!"

Mrs. Owen drags Rachel back to the house. "Let's get you cleaned up," she says.

Frank gets on with his work.

Megan and Joe help him load some
sheep and lambs into the trailer.

He takes them out to the field...

...and lets them out.
Then he drives back
to the lambing shed.

He's so busy, he doesn't see
Rachel creep out of the house
and across the farmyard again.

Suddenly the Owens rush out of the house.
"Have you seen Rachel?" Mr. Owen asks.
"The naughty girl has disappeared again."

"I'll help you look
for her," sighs Frank.

All the children join in the search. First they look in the lambing shed, but Rachel's not there.

"Raaa-chel!" call the boys.

"Rachel gets hay fever," Mrs. Owen explains as they check the big barn, "and she hasn't taken her medicine today."

"She's not in the hen house," says Emily, "and neither is Clarice."

She's not with Jenny and Jim.

And she's not in Debbie and Dina's field.

"Ee-yore!"

shouts Olly.

They cross the cow field, but Rachel's
not there either. And she's nowhere
to be seen in Misty and Toffee's field.

"Where can she be?" says Mr. Owen, starting to sound worried. "Well at least she hasn't fallen in the pond," says Frank.

"Ducks!" shouts Olly.

"Quack, quack!" say the ducks.

17

"Maybe she's in Megan's kennel," suggests Lewis helpfully.

"Well, we haven't looked there yet," says Mr. Owen.

They look in the kennel, but Rachel's not hiding there either.

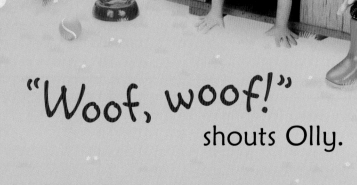

"Woof, woof!" shouts Olly.

"A-tish-ooo!"
"Aaaa-tish-ooo!"

"What was that?" asks Frank.
"It must be Rachel," says Mrs. Owen.
"It's coming from the big barn," says Emily.
"But you already looked there," says Robert.

19

They all hurry over to the barn.

"Raaa-chel!" calls Robert. "You're in trouble!"
"Shhhh," says Mr. Owen.

"There she is,"
says Emily.

"A-tish-oooo!"

"Look at this... A-TISH-OO!
Look at this hen with her sweet
little chicks," coos Rachel.

"It's Clarice!" squeals Emily.
"She's had chicks. I'm so
happy we've found her!"

"Cheep, cheep!"
say the chicks.

"Well I'm glad everyone's safe," says Frank,
"but now I must get back to work."

Out in the farmyard, he sees the
cows waiting behind the gate.

"On no," groans Frank.
"It's milking time again!"
"MooOOO!" say the cows.

Farm words

Bed and Breakfast (B&B) – a place where people can pay to spend the night and have breakfast.

Dairy – a room or building where milk is kept or where it is made into butter, cheese, yogurt and so on.

Hen house – a small building that hens live in.

Kennel – a small house for a dog.

Lambing shed – a farm building where ewes (girl sheep) are taken to have their lambs.

Milking – taking the milk from cows. Farmers usually use machines to help them do this.

Milk tanker – a truck with a tank on the back that collects milk from farms.

Paddock – a small field near a house or stable.

Sheepdog – a dog that has been trained to help a shepherd control where sheep go.

Silo – a tall, round tower used for storing animal food.

Farm quiz

These are Frank's tips for staying safe if you visit a farm. Who doesn't take any notice of them in the story? (Answers on page 24.)

Wear strong shoes or boots, not sandals, and walk – don't run.

Always wash your hands well after touching animals and before eating.

Keep away from places where tractors are working.

Don't touch or eat animal food.

If you get hay fever or asthma, stay away from hay and long grass.

Don't touch any farm tools or machines and don't play in barns.

Don't climb or play on walls, gates, wheels or in animal pens.

Handle animals quietly and gently. Don't chase, frighten or hurt them.

Answers to quiz on page 23

Olly   (chasing ducks, shouting at animals)
Robert   (running in farmyard, not wearing boots)
Rachel   (running in farmyard, not wearing boots, playing in barn)
Mr. Owen   (wearing sandals)
Emily   (playing in barn)

Photography: MMStudios

With thanks to Staedtler UK for providing the
Fimo® material for models. Tractor supplied by Bruder®Toys

www.usborne.com
First published in 2005 by Usborne Publishing Ltd.,
Usborne House, 83-85 Saffron Hill, London EC1N 8RT, England. Copyright ©2006 Usborne Publishing Ltd.